SHOOTING FROM THE LIP

HOCKEY'S
BEST
QUOTES
AND QUIPS

Compiled by
CHRIS McDONELL

FIREFLY BOOKS

A FIREFLY BOOK

Published by Firefly Books Ltd. 2008

Special Edition

Design: Ingrid Paulson
Printed in China

The Publisher acknowledges the financial support of the Government of Canada through
the Book Publishing Industry Development Program for its publishing activities.

To Quinn, Tara and Isaac McDonell-Gordon
and Sue Gordon, for their patience,
love and understanding

CONTENTS

INTRODUCTION

Shooting From the Lip is full of the off-the-cuff comments that keep millions of fans not only watching the games, but also tuning in to see the highlight reels and reading the sports pages religiously. Most of these lines have burst out of the rumble and tumble of the daily grind, from the post-game scrum, the between-periods interview, or over a beer with an attentive scribe. They're fresh, they're frank, and they're all about hockey.

There are serious and earnest comments that bear repeating for their pithy accuracy and insight. Sarcasm, insult and downright trash talking also abound, for the tough, mean and nasty side of the game is as integral to the NHL as its grace and beauty. But colorful tributes and sincere praise are in the mix, too. Just as we all like to see the vain, greedy and lazy get their comeuppance, so too do we enjoy seeing the talented, dedicated and worthy get their due. Hockey players, coaches and management are no different, and the evidence is here.

Is there any athlete more self-deprecating than an NHL player? "It's nice to get a standing ovation in Montreal," noted Florida Panther Scott Mellanby, his tongue firmly planted in his cheek. Mellanby got his round of applause while leaving the ice on a stretcher after crashing headfirst into the boards. There are plenty of other laughs here too, for humor is the glue that binds this compilation together. Of course, sometimes the funny remark is unintentional. "It's not so much maturity as it is growing up," responded Boston Bruins enforcer Jay Miller, when asked if his improved play could be attributed to maturity. Sorry to Jay and many others, but your verbal gaffes have been recorded for posterity.

Over 300 quotations are gathered here, arranged by topic. Speakers are identified by their affiliation at the time the lines were spoken. Unless it is critical to understanding the relevance of the quote, dates have been omitted. Most of these lines are of recent vintage, but some are fifty years old, proving that hockey remains hockey. Goalie Gump Worsley's blunt observation that champagne drunk from the Stanley Cup "tasted like horse pee from a tin cup" is as iconoclastic a comment today as it was in the 1960s. Likewise, Bobby Clarke's admission, "If I hadn't learned to lay on a two-hander once in a while, I'd never have left Flin Flon," resonates as strongly with those of us who know him only as the Philadelphia Flyers' general manager in 2004 as it does with those of us who watched him play in the 1970s.

Whether you're a hockey fan who'll dip into these pages for random nibbles or one who'll devour them in one sitting, cover to cover, you'll find plenty here to satisfy any desire. Bon appetit!

"Every boo on the road is a cheer."

RED WINGS COACH **SCOTTY BOWMAN**

"You're really playing against yourself. You have to learn what you can control and what you can't, and not let what you can't control affect your confidence."

RANGERS GOALIE MIKE RICHTER

"You try to block out all the negatives. You worry about all the negatives, you end up in a rubber room."

SHARK GARY SUTER

"You find that you have peace of mind and can enjoy yourself, get more sleep and rest when you know that it was a 100 percent effort that you gave—win or lose."

HALL OF FAME RED WING GORDIE HOWE

"It's not about what you did yesterday—it's what you do tomorrow. If you rely too much on yesterday, tomorrow is going to jump up and bite you in the pants."

FLYERS GOALIE JOHN VANBIESBROUCK, AFTER BEING BENCHED THE PREVIOUS NIGHT

"In the playoffs, will beats skill."

SHARKS COACH KEVIN CONSTANTINE

"We're going to be the best in the league at something. We're deep in anthem singers."

PREDATORS COACH BARRY TROTZ

"He could deke a guy in a phone booth."

SHARK OWEN NOLAN, ON TEAMMATE VIKTOR KOZLOV

"Great lines in hockey could turn the lights off and know where each other is."

COYOTES GM MIKE BARNETT, ON COYOTES
TONY AMONTE AND DANNY BRIERE

"How you can have a guy who is [so small] dominate a hockey game like he does? He's mastered the art of being able to just stop and turn on a dime and avoid the monsters who are chasing him."

FLYER JEREMY ROENICK, ON PREDATOR CLIFF RONNING,
WHO HAD JUST PLAYED IN HIS 1,000TH NHL GAME

"There is no escalator to success—only steps."

OILERS GM GLEN SATHER

"I'm on the third line. I'm a crasher. I know my role. I'm just trying to help. I'm not stupid enough to think I'm great out there."

MAPLE LEAF DARCY TUCKER

"Some of us were meant to score, others were meant to play goal. And others were meant to do what I do. I tick people off and I don't get danger pay."

CANADIEN TRENT McCLEARY

"We know he is a one-dimensional player, but it's the dimension we don't have."

CALGARY FLAMES GM AL COATES, ON PHIL HOUSLEY

"I have 3,000 penalty minutes. I don't need people dictating to me how to do my job."

MAPLE LEAF TIE DOMI, ON FAN AND MEDIA CRITICISM

"We had too many guys hurt their arms patting themselves on the back. Now, they're probably rubbing their feet from being sore kicking themselves."

COYOTES COACH **JIM SCHOENFELD,** AFTER BLOWING
A 4-1 LEAD AND LOSING TO TORONTO

"It would have been worse if we hadn't blocked the kick after Toronto's second touchdown."

RED WING ALEX DELVECCHIO, AFTER TORONTO BEAT
DETROIT 13-0 IN 1971

"I'm glad that my sons are too young to count!"

NORDIQUE STEVEN FINN, AFTER HIS TEAM'S 10-3 LOSS
TO THE CAPITALS IN 1991

"Well, they were the only two I had."

LIGHTNING COACH TERRY CRISP, ASKED WHY HE
USED HIS TWO GOALIES IN A 10-0 LOSS

"Not if they check the date on the ticket. That wasn't entertainment."

ST. LOUIS BLUE TONY TWIST, AFTER BEING TOLD THAT
THE COST OF TICKETS TO A 4-0 ST. LOUIS WIN OVER
TORONTO COULD BE WRITTEN OFF ON INCOME TAXES
AS AN ENTERTAINMENT DEDUCTION

"My brother Dash hit me on the head with five textbooks in a gym bag."

MAPLE LEAF TIE DOMI, ASKED ABOUT THE HARDEST HIT
HE'S EVER RECEIVED

"At the time it happened, I wasn't disappointed, but I came in the dressing room and I was real upset with what happened. That's blood, man.... Right away I came in and called my parents and apologized."

WHALER KEITH PRIMEAU, AFTER FIGHTING
HIS BROTHER WAYNE OF THE SABRES

"It's a terrible time of year to have a baby. Of course, she got married on draft day, so I think she has no idea what I do for a living."

NHL DIRECTOR OF OFFICIATING BRYAN LEWIS, ON HIS
DAUGHTER EXPECTING DURING THE PLAYOFFS

"He was mild-mannered and I don't know how he ever got into the tough-role business. He was not a rough kid. The rough stuff must have come from his mother's side of the family."

WAYNE LANGDON, CANUCK ENFORCER DARREN LANGDON'S FATHER

"Ah, my sister used to hit me harder."

RED WING SHAWN BURR, ON BEING CHECKED BY DALLAS STAR MIKE MODANO

"I'll still run him on the ice tomorrow."

MAPLE LEAF TIE DOMI, AFTER RANGER ADAM GRAVES (RELATED TO HIM BY MARRIAGE) DROVE HIM TO TORONTO'S PRACTICE IN RYE, NEW YORK

**"Man is that guy ripped.
I mean, I've got the
washboard stomach, too.
It's just that mine
has about two months
of laundry on top of it."**

SHARK **SHAWN BURR,** ON FLYER ERIC LINDROS

"It must be the body. It's chiseled out of marshmallows."

> BLACKHAWK TONY AMONTE, ON POSSESSING THE
> NHL'S SECOND-LONGEST ACTIVE PLAYING STREAK

"Every time I see you naked, I feel sorry for your wife."

> PENGUIN JAROMIR JAGR, TO TEAMMATE MATTHEW
> BARNABY

"We gave Wendel the day off for what is called a body maintenance day."

> MAPLE LEAFS COACH MIKE MURPHY, ON GIVING
> FREQUENTLY INJURED WENDEL CLARK A DAY OFF

"Players today put too much emphasis on lifting weights, low body fat and big muscles that they think make them look good—all that bullshit. What you need to play hockey is heart and determination, and the ability to stay mentally strong. Mental strength beats physical strength any day."

> HALL OF FAME NHL PLAYER PHIL ESPOSITO,
> IN A 2003 INTERVIEW

"They always try to play with our minds. But that won't work with our club. We've got 20 guys without brains."

FLYER BOBBY CLARKE, IN 1976, WHEN THE RUSSIAN
CENTRAL ARMY TEAM PLAYED PHILADELPHIA

"There's a thousand theories, but theories are for scientists. We're too stupid for that. We've just got to get back to the x's and o's."

SHARK MIKE RICCI, ON SAN JOSE'S SLOW START

"I see you finally got a number to match your IQ."

OILERS ASSISTANT COACH BOB McCAMMON, TO MARTY
McSORLEY, WHO WAS WEARING NUMBER 5

"I was young and stupid then. Now I'm not young anymore."

MAPLE LEAF JYRKI LUMME, ON HIS EARLY YEARS WITH
MONTREAL

"You can always get someone to do your thinking for you."

HALL OF FAME RED WING GORDIE HOWE, DURING A
1970S APPEARANCE ON "THE DICK CAVETT SHOW,"
ON WHY HOCKEY PLAYERS ALWAYS WEAR A PROTECTIVE
CUP BUT RARELY A HELMET

"I've said this before, but it's really true: you have to get players to do what they don't want to do."

FLYERS COACH **KEN HITCHCOCK**

"I know my players don't like my practices, but that's O.K. because I don't like their games."

CANUCKS COACH **HARRY NEALE**

"You can't play hockey if you're nice."

LIGHTNING COACH **STEVE LUDZIK**

"It's never boring for us even if there's 50 face-offs in 10 minutes. We don't care. We don't look at it the same way that you guys do."

MINNESOTA WILD COACH **JACQUES LEMAIRE**,
TO REPORTERS

"Maybe one of the qualities
of being a great
coach
is being a jerk.
There are quite a few
of them around."

L.A. KINGS COACH LARRY ROBINSON

"Coaches are like ducks. Calm on top but paddling underneath. Believe me, there's a lot of leg movement."

DALLAS STARS COACH KEN HITCHCOCK, ON HIDING HIS NERVOUSNESS

"This is my third time. They say you're not a coach in the league till you've been fired. I must be getting pretty good."

WINNIPEG JETS COACH **TERRY SIMPSON**, AFTER BEING FIRED

"Just because you can draw it doesn't mean it can happen."

RED WING **STEVE YZERMAN**, ON GAME PLANS

"You can't keep on trading foot soldiers. Sooner or later, the general's got to go."

MAPLE LEAF COACH **PAT BURNS**, AFTER BEING FIRED BY TORONTO

"Everybody's diving now. You used to dive and go back to the bench and guys would bitch at you and say: 'Come on. Don't embarrass us.' Now you get a high five."

CANUCKS GM BRIAN BURKE

"It was a nose dive, a swan dive, a double gainer. I'm surprised he didn't flip backwards in the air while he was doing it."

PANTHERS COACH MIKE KEENAN, ON THE WAY COYOTE DANIEL BRIERE WENT DOWN AFTER BEING HOOKED BY PANTHER OLLI JOKINEN

"It's best just to stay away from him 'cause he's just going to flop and dive. He's not going to hurt me. My daughter weighs more than he does."

DEVIL SCOTT STEVENS, ON RANGER THEO FLEURY

"My old man used to tell me, 'If you ain't dead, don't lay there.' Maybe a lot of guys didn't have fathers telling them that."

OILERS GM **KEVIN LOWE**, ON PLAYERS
WHO FAKE INJURY TO DRAW A PENALTY

"He's going down like free beer at a frat party."

CAPITALS GM PIERRE McGUIRE, ON ISLANDER MARIUSZ CZERKAWSKI'S FREQUENT DIVING

"There's no reason why a player is done at 33, 34. They train better, they eat better, they drink better. This isn't the old days when everybody sat around and drank beer."

FLYERS GM BOB CLARKE, ON SIGNING
37-YEAR-OLD KJELL SAMUELSSON

"Usually, I'm on the bus by now, having a beer and waiting for everyone else. This is cutting into my beer time."

CAPITAL CRAIG BERUBE, TO THE MEDIA, AFTER SCORING ONE OF HIS RARE GOALS AND BEING THE CENTER OF ATTENTION IN THE DRESSING ROOM

"Bud Light."

ST. LOUIS BLUE KEITH TKACHUK, ASKED TO NAME HIS FAVORITE SPORTS DRINK IN THE TEAM MEDIA GUIDE

"Maybe I'd drink a bit more."

HALL OF FAME NHL AND WHA PLAYER BOBBY HULL, WHEN ASKED WHAT HE WOULD DO IF HE HAD TO DO HIS CAREER ALL OVER AGAIN

"The kids just aren't the same today."

CANADIEN DOUG GILMOUR, AFTER ASKING A ROOKIE TO SNEAK A CASE OF 24 BEERS ONTO THE TEAM BUS AND FINDING OUT HE ONLY GOT SIX CANS

"The biggest thing with a scorer is confidence. When you're younger you never even think of it, but when you're older and you stop scoring, you don't walk with the same confidence. You don't have the same arrogance or swagger you once carried onto the ice. You think each scoring chance could be your last, and if you don't score, you're screwed."

BROADCASTER PAT VERBEEK, ON RED WING
LUC ROBITAILLE'S SCORING DROUGHT

"When I was awful, early in the season, it looked like I was shooting at a lacrosse net. Now, it's like a soccer goal!"

CAPITAL MIKE GARTNER, AFTER ENDING A 1987 SCORING
DROUGHT WITH A FLURRY OF GOALS

"It was so long I thought somebody would have to come up with those paddles and shock me back to life."

PREDATOR BILL HOULDER, ON ENDING A 144-GAME
SCORING DROUGHT

"Only problem is I was going high on the glove side."

SENATOR LANCE PITLICK, ON SCORING HIS FIRST GOAL
OF THE SEASON WITH A LOW SHOT TO THE STICK SIDE

"I like to space them out so I can remember them."

FLYER CHRIS McALLISTER, AFTER SCORING
HIS FIRST GOAL IN 94 GAMES

"I'm on fire."

CANUCK DARREN LANGDON, AFTER GETTING AN ASSIST
FOR HIS FIRST POINT IN 32 GAMES

"It's not so much maturity as it is growing up."

BRUIN JAY MILLER, ASKED IF HIS IMPROVED PLAY
WAS DUE TO MATURITY

"I'll be sad to go and I wouldn't be sad to go. It wouldn't upset me to leave St. Louis, but it would upset me to leave St. Louis. It's hard to explain. You'll find out one of these days, but maybe you never will."

ST. LOUIS BLUE BRETT HULL, ON A POSSIBLE TRADE

"I love to play for Pittsburgh. If they can't afford me, then I'd love to play in L.A. or New York."

PENGUIN JAROMIR JAGR

"Yeah, I'm cocky and I am arrogant. But that doesn't mean I'm not a nice person."

COYOTE JEREMY ROENICK

"Jason Arnott will be here as long as I'm here, for the time being."

OILERS GM GLEN SATHER, ON JASON ARNOTT TRADE RUMORS

"The worst thing you can do is **overreact**. But it's also not good to **underreact** either."

DEVILS GM LOU LAMORIELLO, AFTER THE DEFENDING STANLEY CUP CHAMPIONS FAILED TO MAKE THE PLAYOFFS

"I told him to get some blood on it—that would be awesome."

RED WINGS FAN TERI RODRIGUEZ, WHO LOANED RED WING
TOMAS HOLMSTROM HER REPLICA HOLMSTROM SWEATER
WHEN THE DETROIT PLAYER'S JERSEY WENT MISSING JUST
BEFORE AN INTRASQUAD GAME

"I had a [Detroit fan] yelling at me on my own
bench. I was waiting for a [Phoenix fan] to stand
up and do something. I don't want to say, 'Start a
fight.' But at least throw some popcorn on the guy."

COYOTE TODD SIMPSON, AFTER BEING HECKLED DURING
A HOME GAME

"Ranger fans are the rudest and they're proud of it,
I'm sure."

BRUIN BYRON DAFOE

"They don't know a lick about hockey. They never
leave in the third period because they think there's
a fourth one."

PREDATOR TOM FITZGERALD, ON NASHVILLE FANS

"He could rile up the Montreal fans in a hurry. God, sometimes I felt sorry for the man. He must have got a standing ovation when he went shopping."

HALL OF FAME RED WING GORDIE HOWE, ON MAURICE RICHARD

"We're giving the fans their money's worth. We're super-sizing the games for them."

PANTHER PETER WORRELL, ON FLORIDA'S 13 OVERTIME GAMES BY MIDWAY THROUGH THE SEASON

"I'm just glad it wasn't Machete Night."

RANGER BOB FROESE, AFTER FANS THREW PLASTIC MUGS ONTO THE ICE ON MUG NIGHT

"It's always good to have the building filled, even if it's with low-IQ Rangers fans."

ISLANDERS GM MIKE MILBURY, BEFORE A HOME GAME AGAINST THE NEW YORK RANGERS

"We appreciate all the fans that are here, **but w**

eally **respect**

the five or six who stayed with us all year."

NORTH STAR **JON CASEY**, ON MAKING THE PLAYOFFS

"I never thought I'd be an old, fat, ex-hockey player, but I became one."

MAPLE LEAFS GM AND COACH PAT QUINN

"If I'd known it was going to take 25 years, I'd have started earlier."

DALLAS STAR COACH KEN HITCHCOCK, ON HOW LONG
IT TOOK HIM TO GET TO THE STANLEY CUP FINALS

"I've smelled enough sweat. After 61 years, I'm going to give it up. I don't want to stay here till I'm 100. That's too long."

RED WINGS LOCKER ROOM ASSISTANT WALLY
CROSSMAN, ON RETIRING AT AGE 91

"No, I don't fight anybody I played against in Juniors. I think everyone I played Juniors with is dead now."

LA KING KELLY BUCHBERGER

"So my decision, after 16 years, was to walk away now, rather than crawl away later."

HALL OF FAME NHL PLAYER DALE HAWERCHUK, ON HIS REASON TO RETIRE

"Sometimes it could be your legs, sometimes it's your hands. I don't think the brain ever goes. You still have those natural instincts about where to go. I hate to tell you, but I think you lose your verve or your enthusiasm for the game. I think that's part of it."

RETIRED (2002) NHL PLAYER PAT VERBEEK, ON WHEN IT'S TIME TO HANG UP YOUR SKATES

"I'm convinced the head goes before the body. You end up not wanting to pay the price. It happens to every athlete eventually. In a physical contact sport, it shows up quicker. A guy gets tired of hitting or being hit. You can't hide that once it happens."

NHL PLAYER, COACH AND GM BOBBY CLARKE

"He said, 'This is my hometown, can we go?' I said,
'No problem kid.'"

OILER **GEORGES LARAQUE**, ON WHY HE FOUGHT FLYERS
ROOKIE TODD FEDORUK IN EDMONTON

**I don't even like talking about fighting.
It's not an honor. As a kid, I was always
the top scorer on my team. Would I
rather have a good fight or a goal?
I celebrate every goal like it's my last.**

OILER **GEORGES LARAQUE**, ON BEING VOTED
THE NHL'S TOP FIGHTER

"I didn't drop my gloves. They were yanked off me."

DALLAS STAR MIKE MODANO, ON HIS 1997 FIGHT WITH
OILER KELLY BUCHBERGER

"I had a poster of Probert on my wall. When I
fought him for the first and only time, I thought to
myself, 'Great, I got out alive.' "

ISLANDER ERIC CAIRNS, ON HIS CHILDHOOD IDOL BOB
PROBERT

"It's not who wins the fight that's important, it's
being willing to fight. If you get challenged and
renege, everyone wants to take a shot at you."

NHL PLAYER AND COACH BARCLAY PLAGER

"Two people fighting is not violence in hockey. It
might be in tennis or bowling, but it's not in hockey."

NHL GOALIE AND COACH GERRY CHEEVERS

"Lemieux fights like a girl. **He couldn't beat his way out of a paper bag.**"

RANGERS COACH **JOHN MUCKLER,**
ON NJ DEVIL CLAUDE LEMIEUX

**"The truth is
I would never**

spit

on somebody.

I would

punch

him first."

RED WING MARTIN LAPOINTE, ON AN ACCUSATION HE,
STEVE YZERMAN AND SCOTTY BOWMAN ASSAULTED
CAMERAMEN IN TAMPA BAY

"For the most part, with the possible exception of me, I don't think anybody goes out to try to hurt somebody."

FLYER JEREMY ROENICK

"I don't bother people unless they bother me. I just try to give myself a little working room. But if a guy bothers me, then I retaliate."

ISLANDERS GOALIE BILLY SMITH

"Dirty isn't a derogatory word. It's a good thing to be in hockey."

RED WING STEVE YZERMAN, ASKED ABOUT CAPITAL DALE HUNTER'S STYLE

"I'm not dirty, just aggressive. Fighter pilots have machine guns. I have only my mask and stick."

BRUINS GOALIE GERRY CHEEVERS

"I play a position where you make mistakes. The only people who don't make them at a hockey game are the ones watching."

AVALANCHE GOALIE **PATRICK ROY**

"With goaltenders, when they are on, the pucks look like beach balls. When they are a little bit off, they look like BBs."

PREDATORS COACH BARRY TROTZ

"Yeah, the two that went in."

BRUINS GOALIE GERRY CHEEVERS, ASKED IF HE COULD REMEMBER ANY SHOTS THAT WERE PARTICULARLY DIFFICULT TO HANDLE IN A 2-2 TIE AGAINST PHILADELPHIA

"It's like a kid who goes into the woods with his father. As long as I'm close to the net, I figure I'm all right."

FLYERS GOALIE BERNIE PARENT

"Maybe we should hire another coach, so we can push him."

DALLAS STARS GOALIE ED BELFOUR, AFTER HEARING HIS COACH KEN HITCHCOCK WANTED BACKUP MARTY TURCO TO PUSH HIM FOR THE NUMBER ONE JOB

**"How would you like it if,
at your job,
every time you made
the slightest mistake
a little red light went on
over your head
and 18,000 people
stood up and
screamed at you?"**

HALL OF FAME CANADIENS GOALIE JACQUES PLANTE

"I'm the luckiest man alive.
I don't even like the game
and I'm successful at it."

ST. LOUIS BLUE **BRETT HULL**

"How's the game changed in my 15 years in the league? Well, we used to be called hard-working players. Now we're overpaid crybabies."

RED WING BRETT HULL

"It's like the animal kingdom. Adapt or go extinct."

RED WING BRETT HULL, ON ADJUSTING HIS STYLE WHILE CONTINUING TO SCORE GOALS

"I am 10 times smarter than everyone else in this game. Beyond a shadow of a doubt."

RED WING BRETT HULL

"Hullie's a lot like a garbage can. You step on the pedal with your foot and the top opens up."

ST. LOUIS BLUE WAYNE GRETZKY, ON TEAMMATE BRETT HULL'S FREQUENTLY CONTROVERSIAL QUOTES

"A.m. or p.m.?"

CANADA'S STEVE YZERMAN, RESPONDING TO 1998 TEAM USA OLYMPIAN HULL'S CLAIM THAT "EIGHT NIGHTS OUT OF TEN, I WAS IN BED BY EIGHT."

"Fifty percent of the game is mental and the other 50 percent is being mental. I've got that part down, no problem."

ST. LOUIS BLUE BASIL McRAE

"If I play badly I'll pick a fight in the third, just to get into a fight. I'll break a guy's leg to win, I don't care. Afterward I say, 'Yeah, all right, I played badly, but I won the fight so who gives a damn.'"

BRUIN DEREK SANDERSON

"I remember my first year, I hit him with three good punches and couldn't believe he was still standing. He hit me with one and cracked my helmet. My head hurt for a week."

OILER GEORGES LARAQUE, ON STU GRIMSON

"All my friends back home fight on the street, and all they get is arrested."

PREDATOR PATRICK COTE, ON HIS $375,000 SALARY,
MOSTLY EARNED AS A FIGHTER

"I'd rather fight than score."

FLYER DAVE "THE HAMMER" SCHULTZ

"Little Alan Bester, I've often said, has seen more rubber than a dead skunk on the Trans-Canada Highway."

BROADCASTER AND FORMER NHL COACH DON CHERRY

"There is no such thing as painless goaltending. If they could get enough padding to assure against every type of bruise, you'd have to be swung into position with a small derrick."

DON CHERRY

"The people who yell and scream about hockey violence are a handful of intellectuals and newspapermen who never pay to get in to see a game. The fans, who shell out the money, have always liked good, rough hockey."

DON CHERRY

"I don't mind [Pavel] Bure or [Alexei] Yashin. I don't mind Markus Naslund. But if you get Europeans who don't score, they're useless, because they don't do anything else."

DON CHERRY

"I can't hear what Jeremy says because my ears are blocked with my two Stanley Cup rings."

AVALANCHE PATRICK ROY, RESPONDING TO A REMARK
FROM BLACKHAWK JEREMY ROENICK

"Some nights, I'd like to shoot some of them myself."

RANGERS PRESIDENT NEIL SMITH, RESPONDING
TO FASHION PHOTOGRAPHER BRUCE WEBER'S
STATEMENT THAT HE WOULD LIKE TO SHOOT
SOME OF THE RANGERS

"Every time a puck gets past me and I look back in my net, I say 'Oh, oh.'"

FLYER GOALIE BERNIE PARENT, ON WHY HE
CHOSE NUMBER 00 IN THE WHA

"Yeah. Several fans."

> FLYERS COACH ROGER NEILSON, ASKED IF ANYONE
> SUGGESTED HE STOP COACHING WHEN HE ANNOUNCED
> HE HAD BONE CANCER

"What are you doing in this league?"

> CANADIEN CHRIS NILAN, TO FLYER ENFORCER DAVE
> BROWN, WHO QUESTIONED WHAT NILAN WAS DOING ON
> MONTREAL'S POWER PLAY

"Oh, yes, I love sleepless nights."

> L.A. KINGS COACH LARRY ROBINSON, ON WHETHER
> HE PLANNED TO RETURN TO COACH THE TEAM THE
> FOLLOWING SEASON

"Sure, Daniel wears number 22 and Henrik number 33."

> CANUCKS COACH MARC CRAWFORD, ON WHETHER
> HE COULD TELL THE SEDIN TWINS APART

"You'll never catch me bragging about goals, but I'll talk all you want about my assists."

OILER WAYNE GRETZKY

"Some people skate to the puck. I skate to where the puck is going to be."

L.A. KING WAYNE GRETZKY

"It's a special feeling, a great thrill. I owe everything I have in my life to hockey and the NHL. The game doesn't owe me anything. So, something like this is very special."

RANGER WAYNE GRETZKY AFTER HIS NUMBER 99 WAS OFFICIALLY RETIRED

"There should be a league rule where he is passed around from team to team each year."

BRUINS COACH TERRY O'REILLY, AFTER GRETZKY HELPED EDMONTON SWEEP THE BRUINS IN THE 1988 STANLEY CUPS FINALS

"The only way you can check Gretzky is to hit him when he is standing still singing the national anthem."

BRUINS GM HARRY SINDEN

> **The hardest thing for me has always been that I've been compared to myself.**

RANGER **WAYNE GRETZKY**

"What kind of hair did Mel Gibson have in Braveheart? It's warrior hair and hockey players are warriors."

BROADCASTER **BARRY MELROSE,**
WHO WEARS A MULLET, ON THE CONTINUING
POPULARITY OF HIS HAIRSTYLE IN HOCKEY

"I wouldn't urinate in his ear if his brain was on fire."

HALL OF FAME BLACKHAWK **BOBBY HULL**,
ON A LONGTIME MONTREAL RIVAL

"Basically, I don't like anybody."

FLYER BRANTT MYHRES, ASKED IF THERE WAS ANYONE
IN THE LEAGUE HE DISLIKED

"As much as you hate a team like Colorado, you love
to play 'em. The juices will be boiling, and the blood
will be flowing. Let's clarify that: flowing through
your body. Not on the ice."

RED WING KRIS DRAPER, ON AN UPCOMING PLAYOFF
SERIES AGAINST THE AVALANCHE

"Anybody I can't stand to play against, I would like
to play with."

FLYER ERIC LINDROS, ON PLAYING WITH CLAUDE LEMIEUX
AND BRENDAN SHANAHAN FOR TEAM CANADA

"Rocket had that mean look on, every game we
played. He was 100 percent hockey. He could hate
with the best of them."

HALL OF FAME RED WING GORDIE HOWE,
ON MAURICE RICHARD

"At least I don't need a mask for Halloween now."

SENATOR **ANDREAS DACKELL**, AFTER SUFFERING A CON-
CUSSION AND FACIAL CUTS THAT REQUIRED 30 STITCHES

"They had to take a time out to do some repairs to the boards."

BRUIN **DON SWEENEY**, ON TAKING STICHES IN HIS HEAD
AFTER HE LOST HIS BALANCE IN A SKILLS COMPETITION

"Believe me, I know the difference between a stick and a glove. "

OILER **DAVE ROBERTS**, AFTER SUSTAINING A BROKEN
NOSE AND CHEEKBONE PLUS AN ORBITAL FRACTURE
FROM RANGER MARK MESSIER'S CROSS-CHECK, ON THE
NHL RULING THAT HIS INJURIES WERE CAUSED BY
MESSIER'S GLOVE RATHER THAN HIS STICK

"It's still a bit blurry but I can see. I can tell what color the jerseys are."

PANTHER **DAVE GAGNER**, ON GETTING HIT IN THE EYE
WITH A PUCK DURING WARM-UP

"Tell him he's Wayne Gretzky."

OILERS COACH **TED GREEN**, AFTER OILER SHAUN VAN
ALLEN SUFFERED A CONCUSSION AND COULDN'T REMEM-
BER WHO HE WAS.

"It's nice to get a standing ovation in Montreal."

PANTHER SCOTT MELLANBY, WHO WAS KNOCKED
UNCONSCIOUS AFTER SLIDING AND HITTING THE
BACK OF HIS HEAD ON THE BOARDS, ON THE APPLAUSE
HE RECEIVED AS HE WAS CARRIED OFF THE ICE ON
A STRETCHER

"His eyes are wide open and he looks alert.
He might be a goalie."

MIGHTY DUCKS GOALIE DOMINIC ROUSSEL,
ON THE BIRTH OF HIS BABY BOY

"She looks like her mother, thank God."

WINNIPEG JET TIE DOMI, ON HIS BABY DAUGHTER

"Since my kids were born, I put on a shield.
I wanted to keep on seeing them."

MAPLE LEAF ALEX MOGILNY, ON WEARING A VISOR

"My daughter Chelsea, 12, really knows players.
She looked at a book and picked out the cutest
guy and said we had to take this Ilya Kovalchuk.
She was right."

THRASHERS GM DON WADDELL, ON THE THRASHERS'
2001 DRAFT PICK

"He asked me if he could marry Carrie before he
asked her. I said, 'You want to what?' I thought
he was just going to ask for more ice time."

LIGHTNING GM PHIL ESPOSITO, ON HIS DAUGHTER
MARRYING LIGHTNING ALEXANDER SELIVANOV

"**Daddy, you're the best hockey player in the world except that you can't score.**"

CLANCY WILLIAMS, SIX-YEAR-OLD DAUGHTER OF CANUCK DAVE "TIGER" WILLIAMS, DURING A SCORING SLUMP

"**We know that hockey is where we live, where we can best meet and overcome pain and wrong and death. Life is just a place where we spend time between games.**"

FLYERS COACH **FRED SHERO**

"I've always felt hockey was like a disease. You can't really shake it."

CALGARY FLAMES GOALIE **KEN WREGGET**

"Hockey is a man's game. The team with the most real men wins."

CANUCKS GM **BRIAN BURKE**

"You have to know what pro hockey is all about. You have to live and breathe and sleep it. You have to lose a few teeth and take some shots to the face. It's not a pretty thing."

SABRES COACH **TED NOLAN**

"Hockey is like a religion in Montreal. You're either a saint or a sinner, there's no in-between."

AVALANCHE AND FORMER CANADIENS GOALIE
PATRICK ROY

"Our dreams and thoughts were always to one day lift this trophy. When you do it's a fact and no one can ever take that away from you."

OILER WAYNE GRETZKY

"Nothing is permanent in this business until you have the Stanley Cup perched on the trophy shelf."

HALL OF FAME NHL COACH AND GM TOMMY IVAN

"This is the only thing that has seen more parties than us."

STEVEN TYLER, AEROSMITH'S LEAD SINGER, ON THE STANLEY CUP

"If we do win this thing, that Cup's going to be beside me at the altar. I hope the wife doesn't get too mad."

CAPITAL OLAF KOLZIG, ON HIS UPCOMING WEDDING

"Tasted like **horse pee** from **a tin cup.**

HALL OF FAME CANADIEN GOALIE GUMP WORSLEY
ON DRINKING CHAMPAGNE FROM THE STANLEY CUP

"We get nose jobs all the time in the NHL, and we don't even have to go to the hospital."

HALL OF FAME BRUIN BRAD PARK

"The purchase of the motorcycle is on hold."

SENATOR RON TUGNUTT, AFTER SUFFERING TWO
CRACKED RIBS IN A BOATING ACCIDENT AND BEING IN
TWO CAR ACCIDENTS

"I knew I was in trouble when I heard snap,
crackle and pop, and I wasn't having a bowl
of cereal."

MAPLE LEAF NICK KYPREOS, AFTER SUFFERING
A SPIRAL ANKLE FRACTURE IN A FIGHT

"I just tape four Tylenols to it."

OILER BORIS MIRONOV, ON PLAYING WITH A SORE ANKLE

"It's no big deal. Like Gordie Howe says, elbows
are to hockey players what fenders are to cars."

CANADIAN ERIC LINDROS, ON HAVING HIS ELBOW
DRAINED DURING THE 1996 WORLD CUP

"I could hardly skate. I was taped up like a
thoroughbred but I was moving like a Clydesdale."

LEAF DEREK KING, ON PLAYING THROUGH INJURIES

"Fortunately, he only has two legs. He doesn't have anything else to hurt."

THRASHERS GM **DON WADDELL**, AFTER THRASHERS
GOALIE BYRON DAFOE STRAINED HIS LEFT GROIN JUST AS
HIS RIGHT GROIN INJURY WAS HEALING

"I think I might get 1,000 stitches before I get to 1,000 points."

COYOTE **JEREMY ROENICK**, AFTER TAKING
A GASH TO THE FACE

"Most people who don't know I play hockey think I was thrown through a plate-glass window or something."

CALGARY FLAME **THEO FLEURY**, ON THE
500 STITCHES HE HAS RECEIVED IN HIS CAREER

"I was kind of hoping it would straighten it out. One of these times it will."

FLYER **ROD BRIND'AMOUR**, AFTER SUFFERING HIS FOURTH
BROKEN NOSE

"When we think he has run out of incredible things to do, he does something incredible again. You wonder how much better the kid can get."

PENGUINS COACH **KEVIN CONSTANTINE**, ON JAROMIR JAGR

"The only way we could have, was to have shot him before the game started."

CALGARY FLAMES COACH **BRIAN SUTTER**, ON HOW HIS TEAM COULD HAVE STOPPED JAROMIR JAGR

"There are probably four ways to play Jagr, all of them wrong. He's the toughest player in hockey to devise a game plan against."

BLUE JACKETS COACH **DAVE KING**

"Most people have friends, but no money. I have the opposite. I don't have a chance to talk to my real friends, the ones I've had since I was 5 years old. Sometimes I wish I could bring Czechoslovakia to America. Then I would be the happiest guy in the world."

PENGUIN **JAROMIR JAGR**

If you play him like a regular guy, he will bury you.

DEVILS GOALIE **MARTIN BRODEUR**

"**We only speak two languages here: English and profanity.**"

PENGUINS COACH **KEVIN CONSTANTINE**, ON THE MANY
NATIVE LANGUAGES SPOKEN BY HIS TEAM

"He brings something special. I don't know what it is, but if you ask him, you couldn't understand his answer."

RANGER WAYNE GRETZKY, ON ESA TIKKANEN

"He's one of those guys whose English gets worse every year. But as long as it doesn't affect his play, we're all right."

MAPLE LEAF WADE BELAK, ON CZECH TEAMMATE TOMAS KABERLE'S THICK ACCENT

"They say something to me sometimes. But I don't understand all the words yet. So I smile at them and then I go score a goal."

THRASHER ILYA KOVALCHUK, ASKED IF HE GETS VERBALLY ABUSED BY OPPONENTS ON THE ICE

"They do a lot of talking, but I'm not sure they actually understand each other."

RED WING DARREN McCARTY, ON TEAMMATE VLADIMIR KONSTANTINOV AND AVALANCHE CLAUDE LEMIEUX

"Hell, I don't know if he speaks French."

CANADIENS COACH TOE BLAKE, WHEN ASKED IF QUIET ROOKIE HENRI RICHARD SPOKE ANY ENGLISH

"We're scared of losing. That's why we win.
We know what it's like to lose and we hate it.
We enjoy being champions too much."

ISLANDER BOB BOURNE, ON HIS TEAM'S FOUR
STANLEY CUP WINS IN THE 1980S

"It means that we're in the basement."

RANGERS COACH MICHEL BERGERON, ASKED BY A
REPORTER WHAT THE TEAM'S 14 LOSSES BY A 1-GOAL
MARGIN MEANT

"Potential is synonymous with getting your ass kicked."

PENGUINS COACH KEVIN CONSTANTINE, ASKED IF HIS
TEAM HAD POTENTIAL

"Just use the same quotes. It's the same story."

MIGHTY DUCKS COACH BRYAN MURRAY, ON GOING
WINLESS IN EIGHT GAMES

"It seems like we're doing just enough to lose by a little."

L.A. KING AARON MILLER, ON HIS TEAM'S 3-12-0-1 FUNK

"It's the nuts and bolts time of the year and we don't have enough nuts and bolts."

SHARKS COACH DARRYL SUTTER,
ON A LATE-SEASON LOSING STREAK

"A complacent player is a lazy player, and a lazy player is a loser."

BLACKHAWKS COACH DARRYL SUTTER

"I don't order fries with my club sandwich."

PENGUIN **MARIO LEMIEUX**, TO TEAMMATE RON FRANCIS,
WHO ASKED HIM WHAT HE DID TO STAY IN SHAPE IN THE
OFF-SEASON

"One thing I hate is people screaming at me. If you
want me to do something, talk to me. When some-
one screams at me to hurry up, I slow down."

PENGUIN **MARIO LEMIEUX**

"Usually when you play a team, you want to focus
on one line. Pittsburgh is the only team where you
have to focus on one player. When he's coming
toward you, all you see is him."

CANADIENS GOALIE **PATRICK ROY**

"There's no book on Mario. It's not like he has a
favorite thing that he does over and over. Every
time it's a different adventure. And you know that
if he does the things that he wants to do, the
puck's going to go in the net."

WHALERS GOALIE **PETER SIDORKIEWICZ**

His face is so calm. He shows no sign of stress or anything. It's as if he's saying, 'No problem. Relax. I'm just going to beat you now. It's not going to hurt a bit.'

FLYERS GOALIE DOMINIC ROUSSEL

"The only pressure I'm under is the pressure I've put on myself."

RANGER MARK MESSIER

"I started as a fourth-line fighter, went to being a third-line centre, then a second-line winger and a first-line centre. I've played every role there is, and the only thing that matters is helping the team win."

RANGER MARK MESSIER

"When he gets mad, it's like he's in another world. He'll look at you with those big eyes and they'll be going around in circles."

RETIRED (1990) RANGER BARRY BECK,
ON MARK MESSIER

"He ran over a few people, nothing major. Mess runs over people. Sometimes, people don't get up. That's life."

HALL OF FAME NHL GOALIE GRANT FUHR, ON
MARK MESSIER

"Biologically, I'm **0.** Chronologically, I'm **33.** In hockey years, I'm

RANGER **MARK MESSIER**, IN 1994

"If you're built like a freight train, you can't drive around like a Volkswagen."

HALL OF FAME ISLANDER **CLARK GILLIES**,
ON UNDERACHIEVING ISLANDER
TODD BERTUZZI

"It's much easier to slow down a thoroughbred
than have to kick a donkey to get him going."

THRASHERS COACH BOB HARTLEY, ON NOT WANTING
TO REIN IN SNIPER ILYA KOVALCHUK TOO MUCH

"I'd rather tame a tiger than paint stripes on a kitty cat."

SHARKS GM DEAN LOMBARDI, ON OBTAINING
FREQUENTLY SUSPENDED BRYAN MARCHMENT

"It's like he's parting the Red Sea. He gives them an
opening, but most of the scorers wind up drowning."

WHALERS COACH PAUL HOLMGREN, ON SEAN BURKE

"He's like that toy Stretch Armstrong, the one
who looked like he was made of Jell-o."

RANGER ADAM GRAVES, ON TEAMMATE MIKE RICHTER'S
ABILITY TO STOP PENALTY SHOTS

"Hmm, 600 games? What does it mean? It means I'm that much closer to getting fired."

> MINNESOTA WILD COACH JACQUES LEMAIRE, AFTER
> COACHING HIS 600TH GAME

"I just think it's great for David. I think it's terrific. Things like that don't bother me. When I retired, I was third in the league in scoring all-time. If I can live long enough, I might be 100th."

> LIGHTNING ANNOUNCER PHIL ESPOSITO, ON LIGHTNING
> DAVE ANDREYCHUK TYING HIS RECORD OF 249 POWER
> PLAY GOALS

"People don't remember records. They remember milestones."

> LIGHTNING DAVE ANDREYCHUK, ONE GOAL AWAY FROM
> TYING PHIL ESPOSITO'S RECORD 249 POWER-PLAY
> GOALS, ON WHY HE'D RATHER SCORE HIS 600TH

"All that means is that I'll be 783 years old when I catch Scotty Bowman."

> PENGUINS COACH KEVIN CONSTANTINE, AFTER BEING
> CONGRATULATED ON HIS 100TH CAREER WIN

"You want to stick around the league and make a name for yourself. Steve Larmer once told me getting here is the easier part. Staying here is the hard part. He's been right for 15 years."

FLYER **JEREMY ROENICK**, AFTER PLAYING HIS 1,000TH CAREER GAME, ON ADVICE FROM HIS FORMER BLACKHAWK TEAMMATE

"I'd have to answer to my mom."

PANTHER ROB NIEDERMAYER, ON WHAT WOULD
HAPPEN IF HE BOARDED HIS BROTHER SCOTT

"My mom, she keeps telling me she wants a goal. I tell her: 'Hey Mom, I'm tryin', I'm tryin', every day.'"

BRUIN PJ STOCK

"I told her they must all be sold out."

MAPLE LEAF WADE BELAK, ON HIS RESPONSE WHEN HIS MOTHER SAID SHE COULDN'T FIND HIS SWEATER FOR SALE AT THE AIR CANADA CENTRE'S SOUVENIR SHOP

"Optimistically, you hope someday you'll be in a magazine. Of course, your mom hopes it's *Sports Illustrated* or something like that."

AVALANCHE DAN HINOTE, ON BEING INTERVIEWED IN *PENTHOUSE* MAGAZINE

"He says, 'Mommy put me in time out, just like you, Daddy!'"

MAPLE LEAF TIE DOMI, ON WHAT HIS YOUNG SON MAX SAYS WHEN HE'S IN TROUBLE

"I won't miss him. Maybe the West Edmonton Mall will miss him, but not me."

OILERS GM GLEN SATHER, ON LEAVING HIGHLY PAID UNDERACHIEVER ANDREI KOVALENKO EXPOSED IN THE EXPANSION DRAFT

"Lunch is on me."

RED WING BRENDAN SHANAHAN, AFTER SIGNING A $26-MILLION CONTRACT

"Bert's wallet is like an onion. Any time he opens it, he starts crying."

CANUCK BRENDAN MORRISON, ON TEAMMATE TODD BERTUZZI

"Players' salaries have been on the space shuttle and coaches' salaries have been on the escalator."

FLYERS COACH TERRY MURRAY

"I would cry a lot, so I try not to think about it."

HALL OF FAME PLAYER BRAD PARK, ASKED WHAT HE
WOULD EARN IN TODAY'S GAME

"Today I might be making eight or 10 million bucks.
But that's okay. You can only eat one steak at a time,
drink one beer and play one round of golf at a time.
So it doesn't mean you can't live your life and enjoy
it. Money's not what makes you happy."

HALL OF FAME MAPLE LEAF DARRYL SITTLER

" To get my paycheque for two weeks, my family must work 200 years in Slovakia. "

ST. LOUIS BLUE PAVOL DEMITRA, ON HIS
$1.1-MILLION SALARY

"Forget about style; worry about results"

HALL OF FAME BRUIN **BOBBY ORR**

"I believe Bobby Orr had the greatest impact of any player to come along in my lifetime. He earned his place in hockey history by single handedly changing the game from the style played in my day. In my mind there can be no greater legacy."

HALL OF FAME CANADIEN JEAN BELIVEAU

"I don't think you ever stopped Bobby Orr. You contained Bobby Orr, but you never stopped him. When we played the Bruins and Bobby had to give up the puck, it was a good play."

HALL OF FAME CANADIEN LARRY ROBINSON

"The first thing I would do when I saw Bobby coming down at me was to say a little prayer if I had time. I'm sure I wasn't the only goalie who did that."

HALL OF FAME MAPLE LEAF JOHNNY BOWER

"If I can be half the hockey player that Bobby Orr was, I'll be happy."

BRUIN RAY BOURQUE

"I always tell Bobby he was up in the air for so long that I had time to shower and change before he hit the ice."

HALL OF FAME ST. LOUIS BLUES GOALIE **GLENN HALL**,
ON BOBBY ORR'S FAMOUS GOAL TO WIN THE
1970 STANLEY CUP

**"I never knew the rules.
I used common sense.
It's really the only way
to run a game.
If officials called
every penalty they saw,
there would be
no players on the ice
and no one in the rink."**

HALL OF FAME NHL REFEREE **BILL CHADWICK**

"The next time I want to criticize a referee, I'll give 10 of my players $1,000 each and get them to do it."

RED WINGS COACH SCOTTY BOWMAN, AFTER RECEIVING A $10,000 FINE

"I don't make enough money at this point to get into the specifics."

HURRICANES GOALIE KEVIN WEEKES, ON DECLINING TO GIVE DETAILS ON OFFICIATING

"It's too bad it wasn't a brick."

SABRES COACH JIM SCHOENFELD, AFTER TOSSING A WATER BOTTLE AT REFEREE TERRY GREGSON

"It's the first time a ref ever listened to me."

MIGHTY DUCKS GOALIE GUY HEBERT, AFTER REFEREE DAN MAROUELLI TOOK HIS REQUEST, WENT FOR VIDEO REVIEW AND DENIED A GOAL

" **First they give him two,
then it's five,
then a game [misconduct].
I was wondering whether
the electric chair
was next.** "

HURRICANES COACH **PAUL MAURICE**, ON ERIK COLE'S
HIT ON OTTAWA'S CHRIS PHILLIPS

"I was so excited. I was 26 and I didn't think I was ever going to make it to the NHL. I forgot that I was there to stop pucks."

RANGER ED GIACOMIN, ON HIS DISAPPOINTING 1965-66
ROOKIE SEASON

"This is a first."

MAPLE LEAF COACH MIKE MURPHY, AFTER ROOKIE JEFF
WARE NEEDED A NOTE FOR THE TEACHER IN ORDER TO BE
EXCUSED FROM HIS UNIVERSITY OF TORONTO PSYCHOLOGY
CLASS EXAM

"No big deal. I just watched the game. I had the best seats of anyone in the crowd. It was awesome."

RED WING JIRI FISCHER, AFTER DRESSING BUT NOT TAKING
A SINGLE SHIFT

"The first thing I noticed about him was that he was born the same year I was drafted. That's a pretty scary thought."

ST. LOUIS BLUE AL MacINNIS, AT AGE 36, ON A 1999 ROOKIE
TEAMMATE

"I'm trying to act like every other guy, but inside there is a party going on."

AVALANCHE JEFF DAW, ON BEING CALLED UP
BY COLORADO FOR HIS FIRST NHL GAME AFTER
FIVE-AND-A-HALF YEARS IN THE MINORS

"I look out there during the warm-ups and I see Brett Hull and Niklas Lidstrom and Brendan Shanahan and Sergei Fedorov. I'm used to playing these guys in video games and here I am about to play against them for real. It was a dream come true."

MINNESOTA WILD STEPHANE VEILLEUX, ON MAKING HIS
NHL DEBUT AGAINST DETROIT

"We're at the home of one of the richest guys on the planet and he's got one of the best wine collections in the world and nobody's drinking it but me. I look around and the kids are all playing Tiger Woods' PlayStation."

PANTHER STEPHANE MATTEAU, AFTER A VISIT TO THE
OWNER'S MANSION, ON HOW YOUNG HIS TEAMMATES ARE

"I'm not crazy, I'm Russian."

MAPLE LEAF **DIMITRI YUSHKEVICH**

"The Cold War is back on."

> SENATOR SHAWN McEACHERN, ON TEAMMATE ALEXEI
> YASHIN'S AGENT CLAIMING BIGOTRY

"This is definitely the best team I have played [on] in the National Hockey League, but in Russia, the teams I played for were some of the best teams in the history of the game."

> RED WING IGOR LARIONOV, WHO PLAYED FOR RUSSIAN
> OLYMPIC AND WORLD CHAMPIONSHIP GOLD MEDAL TEAMS

"I had a few fights last year, but I need to take boxing lessons. I need to, because in the NHL it's required."

> L.A. KING MAXIM KUZNETSOV, ON ENTERING THE NHL

"There is no position in sport as noble as goaltending."

> HALL OF FAME SOVIET UNION NATIONAL TEAM GOALIE
> VLADISLAV TRETIAK

"Playing with Steve Guolla is like playing with myself."

SHARK JEFF FRIESEN, ON HIS TEAMMATE

"He's the kind of guy who will stab you in the back right to your face."

ST. LOUIS BLUE BRETT HULL, ON COACH MIKE KEENAN

"You hit the head right on the nail."

SABRE BRIAN HOLZINGER, DURING A FIRST INTERMISSION INTERVIEW

"That's a whole new ball of worms."

HURRICANE ROD BRIND'AMOUR, UPSET AFTER DOCTORS
FOUND A SECOND BREAK IN HIS LEFT FOOT

"Getting cut in the face is a pain in the butt."

CALGARY FLAME THEO FLEURY

"We have only one person to blame, and that's each other."

RANGER BARRY BECK, AFTER A LOSS

"That 100-foot skate to the bench after you have been pulled is the longest, slowest skate in the world. It seems likes five miles."

RETIRED (1998) SHARK KELLY HRUDEY,
ON A GOALIE GETTING THE HOOK MIDGAME

"You can probably get a nice song out of those chimes."

SHARK **OWEN NOLAN**, ON THE NUMBER OF POSTS AND
CROSS BARS HE STRUCK DURING THE SEASON

"I have a bull's-eye on my whole body."

PENGUIN **DARIUS KASPARAITIS**, ASKED IF HE WAS
PREPARED FOR OPPONENTS TO ACT AS IF HE HAD
A BULL'S-EYE ON HIS RECENTLY HEALED KNEE

"All my career I've gone to teams on the decline.
I went to Quebec when they were losing the
Stastny brothers. I went to Edmonton after they
lost Gretzky and Messier. I went to Anaheim when
it was an expansion team. I came to Montreal after
they'd won the Cup and were headed down. I was
beginning to think it was me."

SENATOR **RON TUGNUTT**

"Even our train found the injured list. It broke down
going from Washington to Philadelphia this week.
Typifies our season so far."

COYOTES GM **MIKE BARNETT**, ON HIS TEAM'S
INJURY-RIDDLED CAMPAIGN

"The goal is too small and the goalies are too big."

RED WINGS COACH SCOTTY BOWMAN, ON WHY GOALS ARE
HARD TO COME BY

"I'd be lying to you if I said guys weren't afraid
of him. I'm afraid of him, afraid of him running
into me."

PANTHER PAUL LAUS, ON SIX-FOOT-SIX TEAMMATE
PETER WORRELL

"It's got to look funny out there. Me, I'm like a big
giant and Andrew's just a short guy. I heard
they're calling him 'Mini-me.'"

PENGUIN PETER POPOVIC, SIX-FOOT-SIX DEFENSEMAN,
ON HIS 1999 DEFENSE PARTNER, FIVE-FOOT-TEN ANDREW
FERENCE

"He's not big in size, but he's big in heart."

LIGHTNING ROB ZAMUNER, ON TEAMMATE DARCY TUCKER

"The **bigger** they are, the **harder** they **hit.**"

BRUINS ASSISTANT-GM MIKE O'CONNELL, ON
ACQUIRING SIX-FOOT-FOUR, 225-POUND KEN
BELANGER IN 1998

"There are two things I don't want to know: how they make hot dogs and what goes on in the NHL office."

FLYERS COACH **ROGER NEILSON**, AFTER THE NHL WARNED HIS TEAM ABOUT GOALIE RUNNING

"They kept me in the dark and every once in a while opened the door and threw manure on me."

HALL OF FAME RED WING **GORDIE HOWE**, ON HOW THE CLUB TREATED HIM LIKE A MUSHROOM AFTER MAKING HIM A TEAM EXECUTIVE

"We realized if you want to play in the sandbox, you've got to bring your toys."

DALLAS STARS PRESIDENT **JIM LITES**, AFTER SIGNING MIKE MODANO TO A $43.5-MILLION DEAL

"What I've learned so far from researching is that to win the Stanley Cup, you have to make the playoffs."

CAPITALS OWNER **TED LEONSIS**

"How about those quick face-offs this year? The owners can't be happy. Games are 20 minutes faster — hurts the concession sales."

RETIRED (2002) NHL COACH **SCOTTY BOWMAN**,
ON THE 2002-03 "HURRY-UP" FACE-OFF RULES

"Some GMs shop at Nieman Marcus in the summer but I shop at Wal-Mart after the season starts."

THRASHERS GM **DON WADDELL**, AFTER SIGNING
FREE AGENT GOALIE BYRON DAFOE IN JANUARY
AT A BARGAIN PRICE

"One time I was told to go down the hall, past the picture of Cinderella, and turn left. Another time I was told to go upstairs and turn right when I saw Peter Pan."

MIGHTY DUCKS GM **PIERRE GAUTIER**, ON WORKING AT
DISNEY HEADQUARTERS

"**You miss 100 percent of the shots you never take.**"

OILER **WAYNE GRETZKY**

"I don't want to be sitting back and watching other guys do everything."

CANUCK **BRENDAN MORRISON**, SCORELESS IN 16 GAMES, ON MAKING THE DECISION TO SHOOT MORE DESPITE PLAYING ON A LINE WITH LEAGUE TOP-FIVE SCORERS MARKUS NASLUND AND TODD BERTUZZI

"Yes, and I also like jumping out of tall buildings."

PANTHER **JOHN VANBIESBROUCK**, ASKED IF HE ENJOYED FACING 51 SHOTS IN A GAME

"I get pissed off sometimes when it seems like I couldn't get it into an ocean if I was on a beach."

FLAME **DENIS GAUTHIER**, ON HAVING HIS SHOTS BLOCKED

"Branko, you're not going to make a lot of money unless you shoot."

PHOENIX COACH **BOBBY FRANCIS**, TO COYOTE ROOKIE BRANKO RADIVOJEVIC

"As a kid I used to always like to eat chocolate. My mother told me I eat too much candy. She used to hide the candy in the house but I went to look for it."

THRASHER ILYA KOVALCHUK, AFTER HAVING NINE ROTTEN TEETH PULLED BY A DENTIST UPON HIS ARRIVAL IN ATLANTA

"Well, I've got my teeth right here in my hand."

CANUCK MIKE SILLINGER, TRYING TO PROVE TO REFEREE BILL MCCREARY THAT HE WAS CROSS-CHECKED BY MAPLE LEAF JAMIE MACOUN

"I was trying to hit him in the chest. Too bad I missed."

BLUE JACKET SERGE AUBIN, ON KNOCKING OUT TWO OF PENGUIN DARIUS KASPARAITIS'S TEETH

"I was 14 when I lost them [his front teeth]. The main thing was, we won that game, so I was the happiest. You hate to lose your teeth and the game, too."

HALL OF FAME FLYER BILL BARBER

"Daneyko got mad when Kaminski said he was going to knock his teeth out. Dano has only two teeth left, so you can't say that to Dano."

DEVILS COACH JACQUES LEMAIRE, ON A FIGHT BETWEEN
DEVIL KEN DANEYKO AND CAPITAL KEVIN KAMINSKI

"Every time I get injured, my wife ends up pregnant."

BLACKHAWK **DOUG WILSON**,
ON TIME SPENT AT HOME

"He has a great body for a hockey player, too.
I don't want this to come out wrong, but he
has a great rear end."

WHALERS COACH **PAUL HOLMGREN**, ON ANDREI
NIKOLISHIN

"I have to go through a couple pairs of shorts each
game, but other than that, it's great."

COYOTES COACH **BOB FRANCIS**, ON THE TIGHT 2001-02
PLAYOFF RACE

"I don't think it's hypnosis to the point where I'm
going to start squawking like a chicken, but you
definitely feel very relaxed."

DEVIL **KEVIN DEAN**, ON HOW MASSEUR JUERGEN MERZ,
A LICENSED HYPNOTIST, HELPED HIM AND HIS TEAMMATES
EASE STRESS AND IMPROVE FOCUS

"I'd like to thank my parents for messing around
29 years ago."

RED WING **MANNY LEGACE**, AFTER WINNING
THE STANLEY CUP

"Looks frightening from the bench. He's going to scare his kids with that thing."

DALLAS STARS COACH **KEN HITCHCOCK**, ON DALLAS STAR
ROMAN TUREK'S NEW MASK

"I just wanted to see if it was legal, because when he was with us he couldn't catch a thing."

RED WINGS COACH **SCOTTY BOWMAN**, CLAIMING HE
CALLED THE EQUIPMENT COMPANY TO FIND THE SPECS
OF OILERS GOALTENDER BOB ESSENSA'S GLOVE

"You don't want to have a rule for everything, where the book is two inches thick, but if you don't, then there'll be a loophole and the goalies will find it."

RETIRED (1980) GOALIE AND NHL OFFICIAL **DAVE DRYDEN**,
ON PLANS TO LIMIT THE LENGTH OF GOALIE PADS

"I don't like my hockey sticks touching other sticks, and I don't like them crossing one another, and I kind of have them hidden in the corner. I put baby powder on the ends. I think it's essentially a matter of taking care of what takes care of you."

OILER **WAYNE GRETZKY**

"Could you imagine how good Glenn Hall would have been with bigger equipment?"

CANUCKS COACH **MARC CRAWFORD**

"If you jumped out of a plane without a parachute, would that prove that you were brave?"

HALL OF FAME GOALIE **JACQUES PLANTE**, ASKED IF WEARING A MASK PROVED THAT HE WAS AFRAID

66 The top three worst things I've seen in hockey? The invention of the trap. The invention of the morning skate. And the invention of the extremely

ugly uniform. 99

RED WING BRETT HULL

"We've got no-trade clauses. Nobody wants us."

FLYER KEITH JONES, DESCRIBING HIMSELF AND
CRAIG BERUBE

"Really, there are none. We traded him for a
10th round pick in a nine-round draft."

FLYERS GM BOBBY CLARKE, ON WHAT "FUTURE
CONSIDERATIONS" HE RECEIVED FROM THE NASHVILLE
PREDATORS FOR SERGEI KLIMENTIEV

"It's tough for a player to talk about trades, because
when a player talks about a trade that's like throwing
a teammate under the bus."

FLYER JEREMY ROENICK, ON HIS MIXED FEELINGS WHEN
A GOOD PLAYER IS RUMORED TO BE COMING TO HIS CLUB

"If you're winning, you'll be rewarded and if you're
losing, changes will be made. It happened when
I played and it'll happen 100 years from now.

COYOTES MANAGING PARTNER WAYNE GRETZKY, ON TRADES

"I don't care if we lose every game for the next five years and the team goes broke and moves to Moose Jaw. I will not trade Pavel Bure!"

CANUCKS GM **BRIAN BURKE**, SEVERAL WEEKS BEFORE TRADING BURE TO THE PANTHERS

"The kid looks good in his first game."

WHALER **GORDIE HOWE**, AT AGE 51, AFTER 41-YEAR-OLD
BOBBY HULL MADE HIS 1979 HARTFORD WHALER DEBUT

"It was pretty weird to play against Vernie. I went to his goalie school when I was 13."

RED WINGS GOALIE **NORM MARACLE**, ON HIS TEAM'S 4-1
WIN OVER SAN JOSE AND GOALIE MIKE VERNON

"That's great. I'm 100 years old and people are still interested."

ST. LOUIS BLUE **GRANT FUHR**, ON HEARING HIS NAME IN
TRADE RUMORS

"The average guy gets sophisticated when they get older and they get cynical and they think there's better things to do with their life. But not [Gordie] Howe or [Rocket] Richard. They understood that hockey was the greatest thing they'd ever do."

FLAMES ASSISTANT GM AND FORMER PLAYER AL MacNEIL

"He's skating like he's 36 again."

DALLAS STAR MIKE KEANE, AFTER 38-YEAR-OLD TEAM-
MATE GUY CARBONNEAU HAD A GREAT GAME

"I'll never be accused of losing a step. I'm not sure I
ever had one."

RED WING LARRY MURPHY, AT AGE 38

"He's as old as some trees."

MAPLE LEAF COACH PAT BURNS, ON VETERAN MAPLE
LEAF MIKE GARTNER

"I played my age. Not bad."

HURRICANE RON FRANCIS, AFTER PLAYING 39 MINUTES IN
THE THIRD GAME OF THE 2002 STANLEY CUP FINAL

"When no one else signs me."

RED WING CHRIS CHELIOS, ON WHEN IT WILL
BE TIME TO RETIRE

"Only in America."

SABRE **MIROSLAV SATAN,** ON HIS RESPONSE TO THE FREQUENT QUESTION "IS THIS REALLY YOUR NAME?" WHEN HE USES HIS CREDIT CARDS

"I thought they were kidding. I haven't told my dad. He'll be bitter."

RED WING MANNY LEGACE, ON DISCOVERING HIS NAME
HAD BEEN MISSPELLED ON THE STANLEY CUP; IT WAS
LATER CORRECTED

"Luc Robitaille is a great kid and a good player, but ask anybody on the street and they'd probably think Luc Robitaille is a type of salad dressing."

L.A. KINGS OWNER BRUCE McNALL, ON WHY HE HAD TO
BRING WAYNE GRETZKY TO LOS ANGELES IN 1988

"Holezig, Kulzig, what's his name is no Terry Sawchuck."

BRUINS GM HARRY SINDEN, ON CAPITALS GOALIE
OLAF KOLZIG, JUST BEFORE LOSING A PLAYOFF SERIES
TO WASHINGTON

"I was never going to be a player to get standing ovations in a visitor's building. I realized from Day One, the way I played, I'd never be a Gretzky or a Lemieux. Well, a Mario, I mean."

AVALANCHE CLAUDE LEMIEUX, ON GETTING USED TO BEING HATED BY OPPOSING PLAYERS AND FANS

"Not a nice story. Brian Sutter said I looked like Charles Manson. He called me Charlie, then it became Killer."

CANADIEN DOUG GILMOUR, ON THE SOURCE OF HIS "KILLER" NICKNAME

"Being called a frog 20 times a day is something that ends up getting on your nerves."

RED WING MARTIN LAPOINTE, ON AN ARGUMENT AND FIGHT HE HAD WITH HIS TEAM CANADA TEAMMATE ERIC LINDROS BEFORE THE 1991 JUNIOR WORLD CHAMPIONSHIP

"It would be like the Rangers, but we'd be winning."

HALL OF FAME ISLANDER MIKE BOSSY, ON WHAT THE
1980S ISLANDERS PAYROLL WOULD BE IF THEY PLAYED
TODAY

"If you play well and win you're a heck of a leader; you don't win you're an okay leader, and if you don't play well and you don't win, you're a lousy leader."

RED WINGS CAPTAIN STEVE YZERMAN

"When your goalie is sharp, you have a chance to win every game. If he's not, you don't have a chance to win any game."

BLACKHAWKS COACH BRIAN SUTTER

"I think our players need to pick themselves up off the floor and get going. It's time for them to stop feeling nervous and feeling sorry for themselves, and time to go out and play. You play hard, you'll enjoy it. If you enjoy it, you're winning."

COYOTES MANAGING PARTNER WAYNE GRETZKY, ON THE
COYOTES' POOR FIRST HALF OF THE 2002-03 SEASON

"I score most of my goals in the third period because I don't like to lose."

Islander MARK PARRISH